P9-ARE-179

DATE DUE

Demco No. 62-0549

Other books by Phil Yeh

Cazco *1976*
Jam *1977 with Roberta Gregory, Don DeContreras & friends*
Even Cazco Gets The Blues *1977*
Ajaneh *1978*
Godiva *1979*
Cazco in China *1980*
The Adventures of a Modern Day Unicorn *1981 starring Frank*
The Magic Gumball Machine & Company *1982*
Frank on the Farm *1982*
Mr. Frank Goes To Washington, D.C. *1984*
Frank and Syd on The Brooklyn Bridge *1986 with Dennis Niedbala*
Frank the Unicorn in England *1987*
The Penguin is Mightier Than the Swordfish *1987 with Leigh Rubin*
The **Frank the Unicorn** *Comic Book series since 1986*
The **Penguin & Pencilguin** *Comic Book series since 1987*
The **Patrick Rabbit** *Comic Book series since 1988*
Theo the Dinosaur *1991*
The Winged Tiger *1993*
Voyage to Veggie Isle *1993*
Secret Teachings of a Comic Book Master, The Art of Alfredo Alcala *1994*
with Heidi MacDonald

Soon to be published
The Winged Tiger's World Peace Party Puzzle Book Vol. 2-4
Patrick and Hives
Shanghai Waltz, *a true story of China, Phil's first novel*
The Gecko King with Alfredo Alcala

The Winged Tiger's World Peace Party Puzzle Book Vol. 1
Summer 1995
Published by Hawaya, Inc.
P.O. Box 300 Kailua, Hawaii 96734
Copyright 1995 Phil Yeh

ISBN# 0-9644149-1-0

Special thanks to RC Williams for designing the book and to
Tom Luth for making the logo come alive! Extra thanks to
Kevin Sullivan for believing in the Tiger.

The Winged Tiger's World Peace Party Puzzle Book is a fun way to travel around the planet. I'm asking the reader to find the five objects below (an ice cream cone, a book, a heart, a flower that looks like this ✳ and a peace symbol) on each page. You will also see The Winged Tiger on each page along with many other folks celebrating world peace.

This book is dedicated to all of us who can imagine peace. I think of this book as a blueprint for the future. Please share the vision.

Phil Yeh, Lompoc, California • April, 1995

Florence, Italy

San Francisco, USA

Budapest, Hungary

Jamaica

Moscow, Russia

Native American Pow-wow, North America

Istanbul, Turkey

England

Toronto, Canada

Bangkok, Thailand

The Great Wall, China

New York City, USA

Mexico

Munich, Germany

Cairo, Egypt

Barcelona, Spain

Hawaii, USA

Prague, Czech Republic

South Africa

Sydney, Australia

Jerusalem, Israel

The Philippines

Paris, France

Rain Forest, Costa Rica

Bombay, India

Copenhagen, Denmark

Rio de Janeiro, Brazil

Tokyo, Japan

About the author:

The Winged Tiger and a friend in Italy, 1995

Phil Yeh started drawing and writing his own stories when he was really small. He began publishing his own magazine when he was just 16 years old in 1970. In 1976, he published his first book called Cazco. In 1985, Phil started a group called Cartoonists Across America & The World after his friend Wally Amos told him that there was a literacy crisis on the planet. Phil pledged to promote reading and other positive issues around the world for 15 years from 1986 to the year 2000 with the help of Theo the Dinosaur & Friends, Patrick & Rachel Rabbit and a little magical tiger. The tiger stars in this book and will be appearing in a film by Colin Redican real soon. Theo the Dinosaur has been animated into a new CD-ROM by Interactive Ink in Ohio which will be distributed by Panasonic, Inc. in the fall of 1995.

Cartoonists Across America's band consists of some hard working folks including: Richard Dinges, Ted & Trang Lai, Geoff Bevington, RC Williams, Jay Edwards, Kevin Sullivan, and Debra Roberts. Phil is represented by The Starwatcher Agency in the USA and the Winged Tiger is represented by PELI Associates and Trigger Licensing in Europe and by Motoyuki Tomita in Japan.

Phil is married to Philamer Tambio-Yeh, a school counselor, and lives in Lompoc, California. He has three sons, Robyn, Jesse and Gabriel. They all draw, too. Phil continues to paint murals and visit schools and communities around the world - write to us at the address below for our upcoming world tour schedule.

The first Winged Tiger graphic novel appeared in 1993 and featured illustrated introductions by Moebius and Wendy Pini. The Winged Tiger book was 96 pages long and didn't have any words in it - so anyone on the entire planet could read it! You can order copies of that book for only $11.95 + $2.00 postage in the U.S. ($4.00 outside the USA). We will also be happy to send you a fun catalog of other neat stuff (t-shirts, rubber stamps, posters, etc.)- just send us a self-addressed stamped envelope to: Cartoonists Across America P.O. Box 670, Lompoc, CA 93438-0670

The Winged Tiger lands in Bologna, Italy for the International Children's Book Fair in April, 1995